THE
LOST
WORLD

RANDALL
JARRELL

With a Foreword by
MARY JARRELL

and an Appreciation by
ROBERT LOWELL

COLLIER BOOKS
Macmillan Publishing Company
New York

Macmillan Publishing Company
866 Third Avenue, New York, N.Y. 10022
Collier Macmillan Canada, Inc.

Some of these poems were originally published in THE AMERICAN
SCHOLAR, THE ATLANTIC MONTHLY, THE KENYON REVIEW, THE NEW YORK
REVIEW OF BOOKS, PARTISAN REVIEW, and the QUARTERLY REVIEW OF
LITERATURE. "The One Who Was Different," "Field and Forest," "The
Lost World," "Thinking of the Lost World," and "A Hunt in the Black
Forest" (under the title "The King's Hunt") were first published in
POETRY, "Next Day," "In Montecito," and "The Mockingbird" appeared
originally in THE NEW YORKER.

"The Mockingbird," "The Bird of Night," and "Bats" also appear in
THE BAT-POET, a children's story published by Macmillan Publishing Com-
pany; Copyright © Macmillan Publishing Company, a division of Mac-
millan, Inc. 1963, 1964

"Randall Jarrell, 1914–1965: An Appreciation" by Robert Lowell first
appeared in The New York Review of Books; © Robert Lowell 1965.

Library of Congress Cataloging in Publication Data
Jarrell, Randall, 1914–1965.
   The lost world.
   I. Title.
PS3519.A86L63   1985   811'.52   85-3789

ISBN 0-02-069740-6

10 9 8 7 6 5 4 3

Printed in the United States of America
Cover illustration Copyright © 1967 by Maurice Sendak

To Michael di Capua

FROM RANDALL AND MARY

CONTENTS

FOREWORD

The Lost World: Twenty Years After

"THERE IS A TIME . . . ," Ecclesiastes and Shakespeare proclaim, and in the year 1963 the time was ripe for Randall Jarrell to write his first factual autobiographical poems. A year earlier Jarrell was in a poetry block and a year later in a depression, but in the spring of 1963 he had a rush of creativity when he was plucking poems out of the air—literally—from a conversation overheard at the Plaza; from the neighbor's wash on the line; from the bats on our porch. At just this time Jarrell's mother sent him an old Christmas card box from the twenties containing the letters he had written her from California when he was twelve.

In the mornings after that while Jarrell wrote, pillow-propped in the Morris chair, in our second living room, I'd look in as I passed and see that box on his knees and his head tipped down studying a letter spread out on his palm. On the blue-lined pages he had torn from a tablet so long ago were his "Mama" and "Pop" [grandparents] and his loved "Dandeen" [great-grand-mother] and their world out West in the house by the tree house on the street off Sunset Boulevard in 1926.

"Dear Mother," the letters began and usually ended with, "Tha's all. Lovingly, Randall." Within those boundaries Jarrell had packed the daily details of nearly a year of his boyhood. Choosing from these and other details from memory, Jarrell found the bricks and mortar to rebuild that world in four poems.

The boy in the letters went to the Methodist Sunday School and listened to "grand opera" on his crystal set. "Tickets for it cost five dollars. But we get it free. It's lots better than jazz. It's hot stuff," he wrote. Later, "Pop and I explored the Four-Square

Gospel Tabernacle. It sure is nice." And, "Dandeen and I rode the double-decker bus like in New York and went to the new LA library that cost two million dollars. I got an upstairs card." And, "Mama and I went to the County museum. I'd like to spend a whole day there sometime. I liked the animals and bones and weapons best." On the homey side, he reported, "We sure had a good dinner yesterday. We had chicken and squash and potatoes and biscuit and cornbread and lots of other things and peach home-made ice cream and cake. I ate six saucers of ice cream and five pieces of cake." And, in answer to something his mother was checking on, he said, "Of course, I don't bite my fingernails anymore. I'd stopped that when I left Nashville. Why there's not a fingernail on my hand that's even broken."

In "*Children's Arms*," Part I of *The Lost World*, the fantastic and transporting first scene was evoked by this paragraph, "I saw a picture show being made last Monday and Sunday night. They made it in a big concrete bowl and they had dogs and Eskimos and igloos and icebergs and snow in it. They had a snowstorm. They threw Christmas tree stuff in front of an airplane propellor and it looked like a blizzard." Further along in that poem is Jarrell's rapt account of attending *The Admirable Crichton* beginning "*In the black auditorium, my heart at ease*" and continuing through sixteen lyrical lines that sprang from these plain ones: "I saw the Senior Play this afternoon. It is the big event of the term and it certainly was good. It had four acts and lasted two hours and a quarter."

In Part II, "*A Night with Lions*," Jarrell recalls an idyllic overnight visit with his "*young, tall, brown aunt*," who let him lie beside her while her friend's lion "*roars his slow comfortable roars*," and she talked to the boy "*as* [a] *grown-up*" about *Jurgen* and Rupert Hughes, and he thought "*as a child thinks: 'You're my real friend'.*" What a marvel that this elegant translation could be made from these few flat facts to his mother. "I went to Bettie's and had a grand time. The new cubs sure are cute. They're not any bigger than a cat. I played with Tawny. He wants everybody to play with him."

In Part III, "*A Street off Sunset*," when the boy is *forced out of life into bed*, Jarrell is paraphrasing a description from a letter that said, "Instead of giving me the little back room, Mama has given me the bedroom between Dandeen's and her own. It sure is fixed up nice. There are some headphones on the bed so that I can listen to music at night in bed."

This is not to say that these rudimentary phrases contribute to our "understanding" of the poems: after all, we had childhoods, too. But, along with verifying the autobiography, they prove once again with what sow's ears an *artist* can make—what the world says one cannot—a silk purse.

Evident in poems I and II are the boy's love for those who care for him and his gladness in their everyday life: and this is borne out in letters. But in poem III his pre-adolescent anxiety over the wringing of the chicken's neck, the blowing up of the world, and Mama's power over his rabbit's life are not even hinted at to his mother. It took time—thirty-seven years—to reckon with that and to be able to admit his misery at having to return to Nashville. Tucked into the poems are Jarrell's belated apologies to Dandeen and his aunt for never writing them and for trying to excuse this "Because . . . I *was* a child, I missed them so. But justifying/Hurts too . . ." At last III ends happily with the trusting boy on the steps by Pop "at the end of [their] good day."

This aesthetic ending seemed technically correct and was truthful as well, for he had often experienced it with Pop, so Jarrell put away the letters and turned to other poems suddenly crying to be written. To his surprise and dismay he could not find one fit for ending the book, and after thinking about this for some time he wrote "Thinking of the Lost World." Of course it is a limb of the trilogy, but he did not designate it IV, as he wanted to keep it separate, as it is in time. When, like Dumas—whom Jarrell refers to in "Thinking of the Lost World"—he, too, brings D'Artagnan back decades later for another bow, Jarrell bestows another ending to *The Lost World*. Revisiting the scenes of his boyhood, the poet settled in North Carolina and married, finds "The Land of Sunshine . . . a gray mist now

... [his] arrows are lost or broken ... and the planks of the tree house are all firewood/Burned long ago." In accepting and forgiving these changes in happiness even, "Thanking of the Lost World" provides the real conclusion to his boyhood year in California.

Had Jarrell been a few years younger when that hoard of letters arrived, *The Lost World* might well have had more of the bitterness and hopelessness of "Hope" in it. But no: he was fifty-one and the old break was mended. A few years earlier, too, when Jarrell was still undaunted by *length, The Lost World* might have achieved Homeric proportions. But no: it was a time to tighten, to take the discipline of terza rima, and to have done with longueurs. In this time of change Jarrell advanced to new ground: ground not hallowed by Auden and Rilke—*his*, his personal property. How often that spring he'd say to the family, "Just think, Old Ramble has written four-fifths of a book." Reading these poems to audiences, he'd get carried away and confide, "Oh, I just feel wonderful! The way Goethe felt when he said, 'You know, I'm a born writer.' "

All but three of the other poems in *The Lost World* were written over the three-year period before it was published. The new conversational directness of these poems, their contemporary settings, and the increased personal involvement distinguish them from the three earlier, more rationalized and discursive, poems: "A Hunt in the Black Forest" (1947), "Woman" (1953–63), and "Hope" (1958).

In all probability "A Hunt in the Black Forest" marked the close of Jarrell's season with the Märchen on the Rhine. I doubt we would have seen another poem of that kind in his next book. Not so, with "Woman": Jarrell's affinity for her goes as far back as "Lady Bates" and "The Face." In "A Girl in a Library," "Seele in Raum," and "Cinderella" he experimented with portraying women as the observed or the self-observer, and in *The Woman at the Washington Zoo* he perfected the first-person dramatic monologue he carried over to "Next Day" and "The Lost Children" and his later women-poems. When Robert

Lowell praised Jarrell in a letter for his "great parade of women," Jarrell decided to withhold three recent poems: "A Man Meets a Woman on the Street," "Gleaning," and "The Player Piano," for starter-dough on his next book: a book, he wrote his editor, Michael di Capua, that was to be called *Women*.

Actually, Jarrell was in thrall to the feminine mystique, and Life gave him a habitat rich with a mother, grandmother, and great-grandmother; an aunt and aunt-figures; two wives, two mothers-in-law, and two step-daughters. Furthermore, it was no accident that Jarrell taught at what was formerly the *Woman's* College of the University of North Carolina (now co-ed). How could he not have written about women? Oh, but he wanted to, and details and traits from all of us glow and sparkle in his female composites. Jarrell *liked* women, and he meant it when he wrote:

> In the beginning
> There was a baby boy that loved its mother,
> There was a baby girl that loved its mother.
> The boy grew up and got to love a woman,
> The girl grew up and had to love a man.

Was I a source for any of this? Well, yes. I believe anyone married to a writer is fated to see oneself in print: it is an occupational risk a mate must take. Whether it was Venus or Medusa, the Marschallin or Mother Death, many of Jarrell's poems—but not all—have shown me something of what I was for him and something of what I was not. When he exalted my virtues in "Woman," I prided myself, thinking, "How good for him you are, Mary." And when he exposed my vices, I philosophized, "It's only symbolic, Mary. All women are like that." In the Berg Collection of the New York Public Library there are more manuscript pages for "Woman" than any other poem of Jarrell's. This is because from 1953 onward he kept adding everything he could think of and then taking out everything he could spare. He was always enthusiastic about "Woman," and in a version he sent Lowell he wrote, "Nobody will have to read Pope's *Characters of Women* anymore."

I could be wrong, but I don't see myself in the wife in "A Well-to-Do Invalid" nor the blond female in "Three Bills," nor the eccentric in "The One Who Was Different." I believe that "Next Day" is a persona mask for Jarrell's own melancholy over growing older and reacting to not one, but two friends' funerals in one month. While we often talked about our aging and "the meaning of life," this was more troubling to him than to me. I do concede to being the mother in "The Lost Children." The dream of the sunny house in the poem was a dream I told Jarrell, and those were my photographs of my daughters; my feelings about my empty heart that had "lost a child, but gained a friend."

"Write it all out for me, old pet, just the way you've said it. Please?" he insisted: and I did. Then, as was his custom when ideas for poems were gathering, he took up residence in an armchair with a fresh notebook on his knees and an insulating layer of stereo sound around him—Chopin at that time. I remember sitting on the porch with the cat in the pretty weather for several days, sewing the summer covers for some cushions. In due course I heard him calling out, "Where's my magic girl?" And when he found me, he said, "Put down that wicked needle, child. Hold out your hand and shut your eyes. And, I'll-give-you-something-to-make-you-wise." It was my notes smoothed into meter and narrative, and transformed into the poem "The Lost Children."

"The Lost Children" was, as Jarrell said, "sure fire" with audiences. After a reading I would see girl students come up to him with eyes moist from daughter-remorse wanting a copy of That Poem to send to their mothers, and middle-aged women, smiling gamely, wanting That Poem to send to their daughters. How uncannily *right* for them, and for Jarrell, was this poem about a dream, a woman, childhood, and loss. He often shook his head over this, saying in a mystified tone, "Believe me, this is *echte* Jarrell."

A complete departure from *echte* Jarrell are the three nature

poems: "The Mockingbird," "The Bird of Night," and "Bats"—
yet they triggered this book. During Jarrell's poetry block after
1958, he mainly wrote criticism and translated Goethe's *Faust,
Part I;* and in early 1962 he was hospitalized for hepatitis and
could not write at all. Then enter Michael di Capua. Talking
about this in a radio interview, Jarrell said, "I got back to writing
poems again in a funny way. . . . I was extremely sick. For the
first time in my life, I was bored with reading. And Michael di
Capua, who was a children's editor at Macmillan then, happened
to write to me and he knew my Märchen poetry and so on, and
he said, 'Wouldn't you like to translate some Grimm's tales and
write an introduction,' and I said, 'I sure would.' And so I did
different ones. I was gradually getting to feel better and I got
to know him pretty well, and he said, 'Why don't you write
some children's stories? You're always writing about children
in dreams and fairy tales.' And so, while I was convalescing that
spring, I would sit out in the yard where my wife was gardening
and write. I wrote a little story for children named *The Ginger-
bread Rabbit.* And after that I started writing another book half
for children, half for grown-ups, named *The Bat-Poet.* And that
felt just like a regular book to me. You know how it is, you
work all the time on it, and stay awake at night. And wake up
in the middle of the night and—Anyway, by good luck, we had
some bats on our front porch, and I imagined a bat that would
not *write* poems, but make them up. And anyway, *I had to
make up poems for him*—Oh, but in fact, I wanted to make up
poems for him. And a couple of the poems were pretty much
like grown-up poems. Anyway, *The New Yorker* printed them.
Well, by then I was writing poems again and so I wrote two-
thirds of *The Lost World*, and so you can see how extremely
grateful I am to Mr. di Capua." Since *The Bat-Poet* prompted
two more children's books *(The Animal Family* and *Fly by
Night)* and the bat's poems unblocked his own, Jarrell was
overjoyed the day he thought of dedicating *The Lost World* to
Michael di Capua.

That all took place twenty years ago when *The Lost World* came out in March of 1965 and when, in October, Jarrell was struck by a car and killed. And after that? In other words, how has *The Lost World* fared in the real world? It sold out in two years but was not reprinted since arrangements were made to include it in entirety in *The Complete Poems*. Selections from it are continually anthologized as well as taught in classrooms to new generations; and critics are still taking it—and Jarrell— apart.

On the one hand, these poems have been dubbed "sentimental," and on the other, "embracing a wide human involvement." They are seen by some as a "diminishment"; others remark on their "wonderful resilience." Dave Smith writes that Jarrell "wanted things pure and wanted truth expressed. Yet he knew the meanness of the human soul and he was passionate. [This] contention of ruthless intelligence and the justice of aroused compassion mark his poems and keep them forever near me. . . . If you have business to do with poetry and people you have to go to him." Suzanne Ferguson believes Jarrell's work "affirms the worth of individual human efforts to understand and change themselves, and, if possible, the world. Though he sets [his] efforts in his own particular time and place, their impulse is timeless, universal, and transcendent. The world of Randall Jarrell is a world that does not get lost." Robert Lowell said this was "his best book," and it is a boon to poetry readers and especially students to be able to buy *The Lost World* again at a reasonable price. My thanks to John Dixon at Macmillan for making this possible.

Mary Jarrell
Greensboro, North Carolina
1985

Randall Jarrell, 1914-1965:
An Appreciation

ROBERT LOWELL

WHEN I FIRST MET RANDALL, HE WAS TWENTY-THREE OR
-four, and upsettingly brilliant, precocious, knowing, naïve,
and vexing. He seemed to make no distinction between
what he would say in our hearing and what he would say
behind our backs. If anything, absence made him more
discreet. Woe to the acquaintance who liked the wrong
writer, the wrong poem by the right writer, or the wrong
lines in the right poem! And how those who loved him
enjoyed admiring, complaining, and gossiping about the
last outrageous thing he had done or, more often, said. It
brought us together—whispering about Randall. In 1937,
we both roomed at the house of John Crowe Ransom in
Gambier, Ohio. Ransom and Jarrell had each separately
spent the preceding summer studying Shakespeare's *Son-
nets*, and had emerged with unorthodox and widely differ-
ing theories. Roughly, Ransom thought that Shakespeare
was continually going off the rails into illogical incoher-
ence. Jarrell believed that no one, not even William Emp-
son, had done justice to the rich, significant ambiguity of
Shakespeare's intelligence and images. I can see and hear
Ransom and Jarrell now, seated on one sofa, as though on

one love seat, the sacred texts open on their laps, one fifty, the other just out of college, and each expounding to the other's deaf ears his own inspired and irreconcilable interpretation.

Gordon Chalmers, the president of Kenyon College and a disciple of the somber anti-Romantic Humanists, once went skiing with Randall and was shocked to hear him exclaiming, "I feel just like an angel." Randall *did* somehow give off an angelic impression, despite his love for tennis, singular mufflers knitted by a girl friend, and disturbing improvements of his own on the latest dance steps. His mind, unearthly in its quickness, was a little boyish, disembodied, and brittle. His body was a little ghostly in its immunity to soil, entanglements, and rebellion. As one sat with him in oblivious absorption at the campus bar, sucking a fifteen-cent chocolate milk shake and talking eternal things, one felt, beside him, too corrupt and companionable. He had the harsh luminosity of Shelley—like Shelley, every inch a poet, and like Shelley, imperilled perhaps by an arid, abstracting precocity. Not really! Somewhere inside him, a breezy, untouchable spirit had even then made its youthful and sightless promise to accept—to accept and never to accept the bulk, confusion, and defeat of mortal flesh . . . all that blithe and blood-torn dolor!

Randall Jarrell had his own peculiar and important excellence as a poet, and outdistanced all others in the things he could do well. His gifts, both by nature and by a lifetime of hard dedication and growth, were wit, pathos, and brilliance of intelligence. These qualities, dazzling in themselves, were often so well employed that he became, I think, the most heartbreaking English poet of his generation.

Most good poets are also good critics on occasion, but Jarrell was much more than this. He was a critic of genius, a poet-critic of genius at a time when, as he wrote, most criticism was "astonishingly graceless, joyless, humourless, long-winded, niggling, blinkered, methodical, self-important, cliché-ridden, prestige-obsessed, and almost autonomous."

He had a deadly hand for killing what he despised. He described a murky verbal poet as "writing poems that might have been written *by* a typewriter *on* a typewriter." The flashing reviews he wrote in his twenties are full of such witticisms and barbs, and hundreds more were tossed off in casual conversation, and never preserved, or even repeated. Speaking of a famous scholar, he said, "What can be more tedious than a man whose every sentence is a balanced epigram without wit, profundity, or taste?" He himself, though often fierce, was incapable of vulgarity, self-seeking, or meanness. He could be very tender and gracious, but often he seemed tone-deaf to the amenities and dishonesties that make human relations tolerable. Both his likes and dislikes were a terror to everyone, that is to everyone who either saw himself as important or wished to see himself as important. Although he was almost without vices, heads of colleges and English departments found his frankness more unsettling and unpredictable than the drunken explosions of some divine *enfant terrible*, such as Dylan Thomas. Usually his wit was austerely pure, but sometimes he could jolt the more cynical. Once we were looking at a furnished apartment that one of our friends had just rented. It was overbearingly eccentric. Life-size clay lamps like flowerpots remodeled into Matisse nudes by a spastic child. Paintings made from a palette of mud by a blind painter. About the paintings Randall said, "Ectoplasm sprinkled with zinc." About the apartment, "All that's missing are Mrs. X's illegitimate children in bottles of formaldehyde." His first reviews were described as "symbolic murders," but even then his most destructive judgments had a patient, intuitive, unworldly certainty.

Yet eulogy was the glory of Randall's criticism. Eulogies that not only impressed readers with his own enthusiasms, but which also, time and again, changed and improved opinions and values. He left many reputations permanently altered and exalted. I think particularly of his famous Frost and Whitman essays, and one on the last poems of Wallace Stevens, which was a dramatic reversal of his own earlier evaluation. His mind kept moving and groping more deeply. His prejudices were never the established and fashionable prejudices of the world around him. One could never say of one of his new admirations, "Oh, I knew *you* would like that." His progress was not the usual youthful critic's progress from callow severity to lax benevolence. With wrinkled brow and cool fresh eye, he was forever musing, discovering, and chipping away at his own misconceptions. Getting out on a limb was a daily occurrence for him, and when he found words for what he had intuited, his judgments were bold and unlikely. Randall was so often right that sometimes we said he was always right. He could enjoy discarded writers whom it was a scandal to like, praise young, unknown writers as if he were praising and describing Shakespeare's *Tragedies*, and read Shakespeare's *Tragedies* with the uncertainty and wonder of their first discoverers.

He once said, "If I were a rich man, I would pay money for the privilege of being able to teach." Probably there was no better teacher of literature in the country, and yet he was curiously unworldly about it, and welcomed teaching for almost twenty years in the shade or heat of his little known southern college for girls in Greensboro, North Carolina. There his own community gave him a compact, tangible, personal reverence that was incomparably more substantial and poignant than the empty, numerical, long-distance blaze of national publicity. He grieved over the coarseness, unkindness, and corruption of our society, and said that "the poet has a peculiar relation to this public. It is unaware of his existence." He said bitterly and light-heartedly that "the gods who had taken away the poet's audience had given him students." Yet he gloried in being a teacher, never apologized for it, and related it to his most serious criticism. Writing of three long poems by Robert Frost, poems too long to include in his essay, he breaks off and says, "I have used rather an odd tone about these poems because I felt so much frustration at not being able to quote and go over them, as I have so often done with friends and classes." Few critics could so gracefully descend from the grand manner or be so offhand about their dignity. His essays are never encrusted with the hardness of a professor. They have the raciness and artistic gaiety of his own hypnotic voice.

Randall was the only man I have ever met who could make other writers feel that their work was more important to him than his own. I don't mean that he was in the habit of saying to people he admired, "This is much better than anything I could do." Such confessions, though charming, cost little effort. What he did was to make others feel that their realizing themselves was as close to him as his own self-realization, and that he cared as much about making the nature and goodness of someone else's work understood as he cared about making his own understood. I have never known anyone who so connected what his friends wrote with their lives, or their lives with what they wrote. This could be trying: whenever we turned out something Randall felt was unworthy or a falling-off, there was a coolness in all one's relations with him. You felt that even your choice in neckties wounded him. Yet he always veered and returned, for he knew as well as anyone that the spark from heaven is beyond man's call and control. Good will he demanded, but in the end was lenient to honest sterility and failure.

Jarrell was the most readable and generous of critics of contemporary poetry. His novel, *Pictures from an Institution*, whatever its fictional oddities, is a unique and serious joke book. How often I've met people who keep it by their beds or somewhere handy, and read random pages aloud to lighten their hearts. His book *A Sad Heart at the Supermarket* had a condescending press. When one listened to these social essays, they were like *dies irae* sermons, strange ones that cauterized the soul, and yet made us weep with laughter. A banal world found them banal. But what Jarrell's inner life really was in all its wonder, variety, and subtlety is best told in his poetry. To the end, he was writing with deepening force, clarity, and frankness. For some twenty-five years he wrote excellent poems. Here I only want to emphasize two of his peaks: what he wrote about the War, and what he completed in the last years of his life.

In the first months of the War, Jarrell became a pilot. He was rather old for a beginner, and soon "washed out," and spent the remaining war years as an aviation instructor. Even earlier, he had an expert's knowledge. I remember sitting with him in 1938 on the hill of Kenyon College and listening to him analyze in cool technical detail the various rather minute ways in which the latest British planes were superior to their German equivalents. He then jokingly sketched out how a bombing raid might be made against the college. Nine-tenths of his war poems are air force poems, and are about planes and their personnel, the flyers, crews, and mechanics who attended them. No other imaginative writer had his precise knowledge of aviation, or knew so well how to draw inspiration from this knowledge.

> In the turret's great glass dome, the apparition of death,
> Framed in the glass of the gunsight, a fighter's blinking wing,
> Flares softly, a vacant fire. If the flak's inked blurs—
> Distributed, statistical—the bomb's lost patterning
> Are death, they are death under glass, a chance
> For someone yesterday, someone tomorrow; and the fire
> That streams from the fighter which is there, not there,
> Does not warm you, has not burned them, though they die.

More important still, the soldiers he wrote about were men much like his own pilot-students. He knew them well, and not only that, peculiarly sympathized with them. For Jarrell, the war careers of these young men had the freshness, wonder, and magical brevity of childhood. In his poetry, they are murderers, and yet innocents. They destroyed cities and men that had only the nominal reality of names studied in elementary geography classes.

> In bombers named for girls, we burned
> The cities we had learned about in school—
> Till our lives wore out . . .

Or

> In this year of our warfare, indispensable
> In general, and in particular dispensable . . .

Finally, the pilot goes home for good, forever mutilated and wounded, "the slow flesh failing, the terrible flesh sloughed off at last . . . stumbling to the toilet on one clever leg of leather, wire, and willow . . ." There, knowledge has at last come to him:

> And it is different, different—you have understood
> Your world at last: you have tasted your own blood.

Jarrell's portraits of his pilots have been downgraded sometimes as unheroic, naïve, and even sentimental. Well, he was writing beyond the War, and turning the full visionary powers of his mind on the War to probe into and expose the horror, pathos, and charm he found in life. Always behind the sharpened edge of his lines, there is the merciful vision, *his* vision, partial like all others, but an illumination of life, too sad and radiant for us to stay with long—or forget.

In his last and best book, *The Lost World*, he used subjects and methods he had been developing and improving for almost twenty years. Most of the poems are dramatic monologues. Their speakers, though mostly women, are intentionally and, unlike Browning's, very close to the author. Their themes, repeated with endless variations, are solitude, the solitude of the unmarried, the solitude of the married, the love, strife, dependency, and indifference of man and woman—how mortals age, and brood over their lost and raw childhood, only recapturable in memory and imagination. Above all, childhood! This subject for many a careless and tarnished cliché was for him what it was for his two favorite poets, Rilke and Wordsworth, a governing and transcendent vision. For shallower creatures, recollections of childhood and youth are drenched in a mist of plaintive pathos, or even bathos, but for Jarrell this was the divine glimpse, lifelong to be lived with, painfully and tenderly relived, transformed, matured—man with and against woman, child with and against adult.

One of his aging women says:

> When I was young and miserable and pretty
> And poor, I'd wish
> What all girls wish: to have a husband . . .

But later, thinking of the withering present, she says:

> How young I seem; I am *exceptional*;
> I think of all I have.
> But really no one is exceptional,
> No one has anything, I'm anybody,
> I stand beside my grave
> Confused with my life that is commonplace and solitary.

In so reflecting, she is a particular woman—one sad, particular woman reaching into Jarrell's universal Everyman, poor or triumphant. Speaking in his own person and of his own childhood, he says:

> . . . As I run by the chicken coops
> With lettuce for my rabbit, real remorse
> Hurts me, here, now: the little girl is crying
> Because I didn't write. Because—
> of course,
> I was a child, I missed them so. But justifying
> Hurts too . . .

Then in a poem called "Woman," the speaker, a man, addresses the woman next to him in bed:

Let me sleep beside you, each night, like a spoon;
When starting from dreams, I groan to you,
May your I love you send me back to sleep.
At morning bring me, grayer for its mirroring,
The heaven's sun perfected in your eyes.

It all comes back to me now—the just under thirty years of our friendship, mostly meetings in transit, mostly in Greensboro, North Carolina, the South he loved and stayed with, though no Agrarian, but a radical liberal. Poor modern-minded exile from the forests of Grimm, I see him unbearded, slightly South American-looking, then later bearded, with a beard we at first wished to reach out our hands to and pluck off, but which later became him, like Walter Bagehot's, or some Symbolist's in France's *fin-de-siècle* Third Republic. Then unbearded again. I see the bright, petty, pretty sacred objects he accumulated for his joy and solace: Vermeer's red-hatted girl, the Piero and Donatello reproductions, the photographs of his bruised, merciful heroes: Chekhov, Rilke, Marcel Proust. I see the white, sporting Mercedes Benz, the ever-better-cut and more deliberately jaunty clothes, the television with its long afternoons of professional football, those matches he thought miraculously more graceful than college football. . . . Randall had an uncanny clairvoyance for helping friends in subtle precarious moments—almost always as only he could help, with something written: critical sentences in a letter, or an unanticipated published book review. Twice or thrice, I think, he must have thrown me a lifeline. In his own life, he had much public acclaim and more private. The public, at least, fell cruelly short of what he deserved. Now that he is gone, I see clearly that the spark from heaven really struck and irradiated the lines and being of my dear old friend—his noble, difficult, and beautiful soul.

THE
LOST
WORLD

NEXT DAY

Moving from Cheer to Joy, from Joy to All,
I take a box
And add it to my wild rice, my Cornish game hens.
The slacked or shorted, basketed, identical
Food-gathering flocks
Are selves I overlook. Wisdom, said William James,

Is learning what to overlook. And I am wise
If that is wisdom.
Yet somehow, as I buy All from these shelves
And the boy takes it to my station wagon,
What I've become
Troubles me even if I shut my eyes.

When I was young and miserable and pretty
And poor, I'd wish
What all girls wish: to have a husband,
A house and children. Now that I'm old, my wish
Is womanish:
That the boy putting groceries in my car

See me. It bewilders me he doesn't see me.
For so many years
I was good enough to eat: the world looked at me
And its mouth watered. How often they have
    undressed me,
The eyes of strangers!
And, holding their flesh within my flesh, their vile

Imaginings within my imagining,
I too have taken

The chance of life. Now the boy pats my dog
And we start home. Now I am good.
The last mistaken,
Ecstatic, accidental bliss, the blind

Happiness that, bursting, leaves upon the palm
Some soap and water—
It was so long ago, back in some Gay
Twenties, Nineties, I don't know . . . Today I miss
My lovely daughter
Away at school, my sons away at school,

My husband away at work—I wish for them.
The dog, the maid,
And I go through the sure unvarying days
At home in them. As I look at my life,
I am afraid
Only that it will change, as I am changing:

I am afraid, this morning, of my face.
It looks at me
From the rear-view mirror, with the eyes I hate,
The smile I hate. Its plain, lined look
Of gray discovery
Repeats to me: "You're old." That's all, I'm old.

And yet I'm afraid, as I was at the funeral
I went to yesterday.
My friend's cold made-up face, granite among its
    flowers,
Her undressed, operated-on, dressed body
Were my face and body.
As I think of her I hear her telling me

How young I seem; I *am* exceptional;
I think of all I have.
But really no one is exceptional,
No one has anything, I'm anybody,
I stand beside my grave
Confused with my life, that is commonplace and
    solitary.

THE MOCKINGBIRD

Look one way and the sun is going down,
Look the other and the moon is rising.
The sparrow's shadow's longer than the lawn.
The bats squeak: "Night is here"; the birds cheep:
    "Day is gone."
On the willow's highest branch, monopolizing
Day and night, cheeping, squeaking, soaring,
The mockingbird is imitating life.

All day the mockingbird has owned the yard.
As light first woke the world, the sparrows trooped
Onto the seedy lawn: the mockingbird
Chased them off shrieking. Hour by hour, fighting hard
To make the world his own, he swooped
On thrushes, thrashers, jays, and chickadees—
At noon he drove away a big black cat.

Now, in the moonlight, he sits here and sings.
A thrush is singing, then a thrasher, then a jay—
Then, all at once, a cat begins meowing.
A mockingbird can sound like anything.
He imitates the world he drove away
So well that for a minute, in the moonlight,
Which one's the mockingbird? which one's the
    world?

IN MONTECITO

In a fashionable suburb of Santa Barbara,
Montecito, there visited me one night at midnight
A scream with breasts. As it hung there in the sweet air
That was always the right temperature, the contractors
Who had undertaken to dismantle it, stripped off
The lips, let the air out of the breasts.
                                        People disappear
Even in Montecito. Greenie Taliaferro,
In her white maillot, her good figure almost firm,
Her old pepper-and-salt hair stripped by the hairdresser
To nothing and dyed platinum—Greenie has left her
    Bentley.
They have thrown away her electric toothbrush, someone
    else slips
The key into the lock of her safety-deposit box
At the Crocker-Anglo Bank; her seat at the cricket matches
Is warmed by buttocks less delectable than hers.
Greenie's girdle is empty.
                        A scream hangs there in the night:
They strip off the lips, let the air out of the breasts,
And Greenie has gone into the Greater Montecito
That surrounds Montecito like the echo of a scream.

The Lost World

I. CHILDREN'S ARMS

On my way home I pass a cameraman
On a platform on the bumper of a car
Inside which, rolling and plunging, a comedian
Is working; on one white lot I see a star
Stumble to her igloo through the howling gale
Of the wind machines. On Melrose a dinosaur
And pterodactyl, with their immense pale
Papier-mâché smiles, look over the fence
Of *The Lost World*.
                   Whispering to myself the tale
These shout—done with my schoolwork, I commence
My real life: my arsenal, my workshop
Opens, and in impotent omnipotence
I put on the helmet and the breastplate Pop
Cut out and soldered for me. Here is the shield
I sawed from beaver board and painted; here on top
The bow that only Odysseus can wield
And eleven vermilion-ringed, goose-feathered arrows.
(The twelfth was broken on the battlefield
When, searching among snap beans and potatoes,
I stepped on it.) Some dry weeds, a dead cane
Are my spears. The knife on the bureau's
My throwing-knife; the small unpainted biplane
Without wheels—that so often, helped by human hands,
Has taken off from, landed on, the counterpane—
Is my Spad.
          O dead list, that misunderstands

And laughs at and lies about the new live wild
Loves it lists! that sets upright, in the sands
Of age in which nothing grows, where all our friends
    are old,
A few dried leaves marked THIS IS THE GREEN-
    WOOD—
O arms that arm, for a child's wars, the child!

And yet they are good, if anything is good,
Against his enemies . . . Across the seas
At the bottom of the world, where Childhood
Sits on its desert island with Achilles
And Pitamakan, the White Blackfoot:
In the black auditorium, my heart at ease,
I watch the furred castaways (the seniors put
A play on every spring) tame their wild beasts,
Erect their tree house. Chatting over their fruit,
Their coconuts, they relish their stately feasts.
The family's servant, their magnanimous
Master now, rules them by right. Nature's priests,
They worship at Nature's altar; when with decorous
Affection the Admirable Crichton
Kisses a girl like a big Wendy, all of us
Squirm or sit up in our seats . . . Undone
When an English sail is sighted, the prisoners
Escape from their Eden to the world: the real one
Where servants are servants, masters masters,
And no one's magnanimous. The lights go on
And we go off, robbed of our fruit, our furs—
The island that the children ran is gone.

The island sang to me: *Believe! Believe!*
And didn't I know a lady with a lion?
Each evening, as the sun sank, didn't I grieve

To leave *my* tree house for reality?
There was nothing there for me to disbelieve.
At peace among my weapons, I sit in my tree
And feel: *Friday night, then Saturday, then Sunday!*

I'm dreaming of a wolf, as Mama wakes me,
And a tall girl who is—outside it's gray,
I can't remember, I jump up and dress.
We eat in the lighted kitchen. And what is play
For me, for them is habit. Happiness
Is a quiet presence, breathless and familiar:
My grandfather and I sit there in oneness
As the Sunset bus, lit by the lavender
And rose of sunrise, takes us to the dark
Echoing cavern where Pop, a worker,
Works for our living. As he rules a mark,
A short square pencil in his short square hand,
On a great sheet of copper, I make some remark
He doesn't hear. In that hard maze—in that land
That grown men live in—in the world of work,
He measures, shears, solders; and I stand
Empty-handed, watching him. I wander into the murk
The naked light bulbs pierce: the workmen, making
  something,
Say something to the boy in his white shirt. I jerk
As the sparks fly at me. The man hammering
As acid hisses, and the solder turns to silver,
Seems to me a dwarf hammering out the Ring
In the world under the world. The hours blur;
Bored and not bored, I bend things out of lead.
I wash my smudged hands, as my grandfather
Washes his black ones, with their gritty soap: ahead,
Past their time clock, their pay window, is the blue

And gold and white of noon. The sooty thread
Up which the laborers feel their way into
Their wives and houses, is money; the fact of life,
The secret the grown-ups share, is what to do
To make money. The husband Adam, Eve his wife
Have learned how not to have to do without
Till Santa Claus brings them their Boy Scout knife—
Nor do they find things in dreams, carry a paper route,
Sell Christmas seals . . .

                  Starting *his* Saturday, his Sunday,
Pop tells me what I love to hear about,
His boyhood in Shelbyville. I play
What he plays, hunt what he hunts, remember
What he remembers: it seems to me I could stay
In that dark forest, lit by one fading ember
Of his campfire, forever . . . But we're home.
I run in love to each familiar member
Of this little state, clustered about the Dome
Of St. Nicholas—this city in which my rabbit
Depends on me, and I on everyone—this first Rome
Of childhood, so absolute in every habit
That when we hear the world our jailor say:
"Tell me, art thou a Roman?" the time we inhabit
Drops from our shoulders, and we answer: "Yea.
I stand at Caesar's judgment seat, I appeal
Unto Caesar."

              I wash my hands, Pop gives his pay
Envelope to Mama; we sit down to our meal.
The phone rings: Mrs. Mercer wonders if I'd care
To go to the library. That would be ideal,
I say when Mama lets me. I comb my hair
And find the four books I have out: *The Food
Of the Gods* was best. Liking that world where

The children eat, and grow giant and good,
I swear as I've often sworn: "*I'll* never forget
What it's like, when *I've* grown up." A prelude
By Chopin, hammered note by note, like alphabet
Blocks, comes from next door. It's played with real
   feeling,
The feeling of being indoors practicing. "And yet
It's not as if—" a gray electric, stealing
To the curb on silent wheels, has come; and I
See on the back seat (sight more appealing
Than any human sight!) my own friend Lucky,
Half wolf, half police-dog. And he can play the piano—
Play that he does, that is—and jump so high
For a ball that he turns a somersault. "Hello,"
I say to the lady, and hug Lucky . . . In my
Talk with the world, in which it tells me what I
   know
And I tell it, "I know—" how strange that I
Know nothing, and yet it tells me what I know!—
I appreciate the animals, who stand by
Purring. Or else they sit and pant. It's so—
So *agreeable*. If only people purred and panted!
So, now, Lucky and I sit in our row,
Mrs. Mercer in hers. I take for granted
The tiller by which she steers, the yellow roses
In the bud vases, the whole enchanted
Drawing room of our progress. The glass encloses
As glass does, a womanish and childish
And doggish universe. We press our noses
To the glass and wish: the angel- and devilfish
Floating by on Vine, on Sunset, shut their eyes
And press their noses to their glass and wish.

II. A NIGHT WITH LIONS

When I was twelve we'd visit my aunt's friend
Who owned a lion, the Metro-Goldwyn-Mayer
Lion. I'd play with him, and he'd pretend
To play with me. I was the real player
But he'd trot back and forth inside his cage
Till he got bored. I put Tawny in the prayer
I didn't believe in, not at my age,
But said still; just as I did everything in fours
And gave to Something, on the average,
One cookie out of three. And by my quartz, my ores,
My wood with the bark on it, from the Petrified
Forest, I put his dewclaw . . .
                              Now the lion roars
His slow comfortable roars; I lie beside
My young, tall, brown aunt, out there in the past
Or future, and I sleepily confide
My dream-discovery: my breath comes fast
Whenever I see someone with your skin,
Hear someone with your voice. The lion's steadfast
Roar goes on in the darkness. I have been
Asleep a while when I remember: you
Are—you, and Tawny was the lion in—
In *Tarzan*. In *Tarzan!* Just as we used to,
I talk to you, you talk to me or pretend
To talk to me as grown-up people do,
Of *Jurgen* and Rupert Hughes, till in the end
I think as a child thinks: "You're my real friend."

III. A STREET OFF SUNSET

Sometimes as I drive by the factory
That manufactures, after so long, Vicks
VapoRub Ointment, there rises over me
A eucalyptus tree. I feel its stair-sticks
Impressed on my palms, my insteps, as I climb
To my tree house. The gray leaves make me mix
My coughing chest, anointed at bedtime,
With the smell of the sap trickling from the tan
Trunk, where the nails go in.
                                    My lifetime
Got rid of, I sit in a dark blue sedan
Beside my great-grandmother, in Hollywood.
We pass a windmill, a pink sphinx, an Allbran
Billboard; thinking of Salâmmbo, Robin Hood,
The old prospector with his flapjack in the air,
I sit with my hands folded: I am good.

That night as I lie crossways in an armchair
Reading *Amazing Stories* (just as, long before,
I'd lie by my rich uncle's polar bear
On his domed library's reflecting floor
In the last year of the first World War, and see
A poor two-seater being attacked by four
Triplanes, on the cover of the *Literary
Digest*, and a Camel coming to its aid;
I'd feel the bear's fur warm and rough against me,
The colors of the afternoon would fade,
I'd reach into the bear's mouth and hold tight
To its front tooth and think, "I'm not afraid")
There off Sunset, in the lamplit starlight,

A scientist is getting ready to destroy
The world. "It's time for you to say good night,"
Mama tells me; I go on in breathless joy.
"Remember, tomorrow is a school day,"
Mama tells me; I go on in breathless joy.

At last I go to Mama in her gray
Silk, to Pop, to Dandeen in her black
Silk. I put my arms around them, they
Put their arms around me. Then I go back
To my bedroom; I read as I undress.
The scientist is ready to attack.
Mama calls, "Is your light out?" I call back, "Yes,"
And turn the light out. Forced out of life into
Bed, for a moment I lie comfortless
In the blank darkness; then as I always do,
I put on the earphones of the crystal set—
Each bed has its earphones—and the uneasy tissue
Of their far-off star-sound, of the blue-violet
Of space, surrounds the sweet voice from the Tabernacle
Of the Four-Square Gospel. A vague marionette,
Tall, auburn, holds her arms out, to unshackle
The bonds of sin, of sleep—as, next instant, the sun
Holds its arms out through the fig, the lemon tree,
In the back yard the clucking hens all cackle
As Mama brings their chicken feed. I see
My magazine. My magazine! Dressing for school,
I read how the good world wins its victory
Over that bad man. Books; book strap; jump the footstool
You made in Manual Training . . . Then we three
Sit down, and one says grace; and then, by rule,
By that habit that moves the stars, some coffee—
One spoonful—is poured out into my milk

And the milk, transubstantiated, is coffee.
And Mama's weekday wash-dress, Dandeen's soft black silk
Are ways that habit itself makes holy
Just as, on Sunday mornings, Wednesday nights, His will
Comes in their ways—of Church, of Prayer Meeting—to set
   free
The spirit from the flesh it questions.
                                    So,
So unquestioned, my own habit moves me
To and through and from school, like a domino,
Till, home, I wake to find that I am playing
Dominoes with Dandeen. Her old face is slow
In pleasure, slow in doubt, as she sits weighing
Strategies: patient, equable, and humble,
She hears what this last child of hers is saying
In pride or bewilderment; and she will grumble
Like a child or animal when, indifferent
To the reasons of my better self, I mumble:
"I'd better stop now—the rabbit . . ."
                                 I relent
And play her one more game. It *is* miraculous
To have a great-grandmother: I feel different
From others as, between moves, we discuss
The War Between the States. The cheerful troops
Ride up to our farmhouse, steal from us
The spoons, the horses—when their captain stoops
To Dandeen and puts Dandeen on his horse,
She cries . . . As I run by the chicken coops
With lettuce for my rabbit, real remorse
Hurts me, here, now: the little girl is crying
Because I didn't write. Because—
                              of course,
I *was* a child, I missed them so. But justifying

17

Hurts too: if only I could play you one more game,
See you all one more time! I think of you dying
Forgiving me—or not, it is all the same
To the forgiven . . . My rabbit's glad to see me;
He scrambles to me, gives me little tame
Bites before he eats the lettuce. His furry
Long warm soft floppy ears, his crinkling nose
Are reassuring to a child. They guarantee,
As so much here does, that the child knows
Who takes care of him, whom he takes care of.

Mama comes out and takes in the clothes
From the clothesline. She looks with righteous love
At all of us, her spare face half a girl's.
She enters a chicken coop, and the hens shove
And flap and squawk, in fear; the whole flock whirls
Into the farthest corner. She chooses one,
Comes out, and wrings its neck. The body hurls
Itself out—lunging, reeling, it begins to run
Away from Something, to fly away from Something
In great flopping circles. Mama stands like a nun
In the center of each awful, anguished ring.
The thudding and scrambling go on, go on—then they fade,
I open my eyes, it's over . . . Could such a thing
Happen to anything? It could to a rabbit, I'm afraid;
It could to—
            "Mama, you won't kill Reddy ever,
You won't ever, will you?" The farm woman tries to
   persuade
The little boy, her grandson, that she'd never
Kill the boy's rabbit, never even think of it.
He would like to believe her . . . And whenever
I see her, there in that dark infinite,

Standing like Judith, with the hen's head in her hand,
I explain it away, in vain—a hypocrite,
Like all who love.
                              Into the blue wonderland
Of Hollywood, the sun sinks, past the eucalyptus,
The sphinx, the windmill, and I watch and read and
Hold my story tight. And when the bus
Stops at the corner and Pop—Pop!—steps down
And I run out to meet him, a blurred nimbus,
Half-red, half-gold, enchants his sober brown
Face, his stooped shoulders, into the All-Father's.
He tells me about the work he's done downtown,
We sit there on the steps. My universe
Mended almost, I tell him about the scientist. I say,
"He couldn't really, could he, Pop?" My comforter's
Eyes light up, and he laughs. "No, that's just play,
Just make-believe," he says. The sky is gray,
We sit there, at the end of our good day.

A WELL-TO-DO INVALID

When you first introduced me to your nurse
I thought: "She's like your wife." I mean, I thought:
"She's like your nurse—" it was your wife.

She gave this old friend of her husband's
A pale ingratiating smile; we talked
And she agreed with me about everything.
I thought: "She's quite agreeable."
You gave a pleased laugh—you were feeling good.
She laughed and agreed with you.

                        I said to her
—That is, I didn't say to her: "You liar!"
She held out
Her deck of smiles, I cut, and she dealt.

Almost as the years have sprung up, fallen back,
I've seen you in and out of bed; meanwhile,
Hovering solicitously alongside,
This governess, this mother
In her off-whites—pretty as a nurse
Is thinly and efficiently and optimistically
Pretty—has spoken with an enthusiasm
Like winter sunlight, of the comprehensiveness of insurance.
If you want it to, it can cover anything.

Like the governor on an engine, she has governed
Your rashness. And how many sins
She has forgiven in her big child! How many times
She has telephoned in an emergency
For the right specialist!

After I'd left your bed she'd take me to the door
And tell me about your heart and bowels.
When you were up and talking she would listen
A long time, oh so long! but go to bed
Before we did, with a limp, wan, almost brave
"Goodnight!" You are a natural
Disaster she has made her own. Meanly
Clinging to you, taking care—all praise
And understanding outside, and inside all insurance—
She has stood by you like a plaster Joan of Arc.
Prematurely tired, prematurely
Mature, she has endured
Much, indulgently
Repeating like a piece of white carbon paper
The opinions of that boisterous, sick thing, a man.
I can see through her—but then, who can't?
Her dishonesty is so transparent
It has about it a kind of honesty.
She has never once said what she thought, done what she
        wanted,
But (as if invented by some old economist
And put on an island, to trade with her mate)
Has acted in impersonal self-interest.

Never to do one thing for its own sake!

Year in, year out, with what sincerity
You said anything, demanded everything,
And she, the liar!
Was good to you—oh, insincerely good,
Good for all the worst reasons. Good.
And she was nice to me, and I was nice
To her: I *wanted* to be nice to her.

She was wrong, and I was right, and I was sick of it.
It wasn't right for her always to be wrong
And work so hard and get so little: I felt guilty
Because I wasn't on her side. I was on her side.

It was a terrible shock to me when she died.
I saw her cheeks red for the first time
Among the snowdrifts covering her coffin;
And you were up and talking, well with grief.
As I realized how easily you'd fill
This vacancy, I was sorry
For you and for that pale self-sufficient ghost
That had tended so long your self-sufficiency.

THE X-RAY WAITING ROOM
IN THE HOSPITAL

I am dressed in my big shoes and wrinkled socks
And one of the light blue, much-laundered smocks
The men and women of this country wear.
All of us miss our own underwear
And the old days. These new, plain, mean
Days of pain and care, this routine
Misery has made us into cases, the one case
The one doctor cures forever . . . The face
The patients have in common hopes without hope
For something from outside the machine—its wife,
Its husband—to burst in and hand it life;
But when the door opens, it's another smock.
It looks at us, we look at it. Our little flock
Of blue-smocked sufferers, in naked equality,
Longs for each nurse and doctor who goes by
Well and dressed, to make friends with, single out, the *I*
That used to be, but we are indistinguishable.
It is better to lie flat upon a table,
A dye in my spine. The roentgenologist
Introduces me to a kind man, a specialist
In spines like mine: the lights go out, he rotates me.
My myelogram is negative. This elates me,
The good-humored specialist congratulates me,
And I take off my smock in joy, put on
My own pajamas, my own dressing gown,
And ride back to my own room, 601.

IN GALLERIES

The guard has a right to despair. He stands by God
Being tickled by the Madonna; the baby laughs
And pushes himself away from his mother.
The lines and hollows of the piece of stone
Are human to people: their hearts go out to it.
But the guard has no one to make him human—
They walk through him as if he were a reflection.
The guard does not see them either, you are sure,
But he notices when someone touches something
And tells him not to; otherwise he stands
Blind, silent, among the people who go by
Indistinguishably, like minutes, like the hours.
Slowly the days go by, the years go by
Quickly: how many minutes does it take
To make a guard's hair uniformly gray?

But in Italy, sometimes, a guard is different.
He is poorer than a guard would be at home—
How cheap his old uniform is, how dirty!
He is a fountain of Italian:
He pulls back a curtain, shows you where to stand,
Cajoles you back to the Ludovisi Throne
To show you the side people forget to look at—
And exclaiming hopefully, vivaciously,
Bellissima! he shows you that in the smashed
Head of the crouching Venus the untouched lips
Are still parted hopefully, vivaciously,
In a girl's clear smile. He speaks and smiles;
And whether or not you understand Italian,
You understand he is human, and still hopes—

And, smiling, repeating his *Bellissima!*
You give him a dime's worth of aluminum.

You may even see a guard who is dumb, whose rapt
Smile, curtain-pulling-back, place-indication,
Plain conviction that he guards a miracle
Are easier to understand than Italian.
His gestures are full of faith in—of faith.
When at last he takes a magnifying glass
From the shiny pocket of his uniform
And shows you that in the painting of a woman
Who holds in her arms the death of the world
The something on the man's arm is the woman's
Tear, you and the man and the woman and the guard
Are dumbly one. You say *Bellissima!*
Bellissima! and give him his own rapt,
Dumb, human smile, convinced he guards
A miracle. Leaving, you hand the man
A quarter's worth of nickel and aluminum.

WELL WATER

What a girl called "the dailiness of life"
(Adding an errand to your errand. Saying,
"Since you're up . . ." Making you a means to
A means to a means to) is well water
Pumped from an old well at the bottom of the world.
The pump you pump the water from is rusty
And hard to move and absurd, a squirrel-wheel
A sick squirrel turns slowly, through the sunny
Inexorable hours. And yet sometimes
The wheel turns of its own weight, the rusty
Pump pumps over your sweating face the clear
Water, cold, so cold! you cup your hands
And gulp from them the dailiness of life.

THE LOST CHILDREN

Two little girls, one fair, one dark,
One alive, one dead, are running hand in hand
Through a sunny house. The two are dressed
In red and white gingham, with puffed sleeves and sashes.
They run away from me . . . But I am happy;
When I wake I feel no sadness, only delight.
I've seen them again, and I am comforted
That, somewhere, they still are.

It is strange
To carry inside you someone else's body;
To know it before it's born;
To see at last that it's a boy or girl, and perfect;
To bathe it and dress it; to watch it
Nurse at your breast, till you almost know it
Better than you know yourself—better than it knows itself.
You own it as you made it.
You are the authority upon it.

But as the child learns
To take care of herself, you know her less.
Her accidents, adventures are her own,
You lose track of them. Still, you know more
About her than anyone *except* her.

Little by little the child in her dies.
You say, "I have lost a child, but gained a friend."
You feel yourself gradually discarded.
She argues with you or ignores you
Or is kind to you. She who begged to follow you

Anywhere, just so long as it was you,
Finds follow the leader no more fun.
She makes few demands; you are grateful for the few.

The young person who writes once a week
Is the authority upon herself.
She sits in my living room and shows her husband
My albums of her as a child. He enjoys them
And makes fun of them. I look too
And I realize the girl in the matching blue
Mother-and-daughter dress, the fair one carrying
The tin lunch box with the half-pint thermos bottle
Or training her pet duck to go down the slide
Is lost just as the dark one, who is dead, is lost.
But the world in which the two wear their flared coats
And the hats that match, exists so uncannily
That, after I've seen its pictures for an hour,
I believe in it: the bandage coming loose
One has in the picture of the other's birthday,
The castles they are building, at the beach for asthma.
I look at them and all the old sure knowledge
Floods over me, when I put the album down
I keep saying inside: "I *did* know those children.
I braided those braids. I was driving the car
The day that she stepped in the can of grease
We were taking to the butcher for our ration points.
I *know* those children. I know all about them.
Where are they?"

I stare at her and try to see some sign
Of the child she was. I can't believe there isn't any.
I tell her foolishly, pointing at the picture,

That I keep wondering where she is.
She tells me, "Here I am."
                              Yes, and the other
Isn't dead, but has everlasting life . . .

The girl from next door, the borrowed child,
Said to me the other day, "You like children so much,
Don't you want to have some of your own?"
I couldn't believe that she could say it.
I thought: "Surely you can look at me and see them."

When I see them in my dreams I feel such joy.
If I could dream of them every night!

When I think of my dream of the little girls
It's as if we were playing hide-and-seek.
The dark one
Looks at me longingly, and disappears;
The fair one stays in sight, just out of reach
No matter where I reach. I am tired
As a mother who's played all day, some rainy day.
I don't want to play it any more, I don't want to,
But the child keeps on playing, so I play.

THREE BILLS

Once at the Plaza, looking out into the park
Past the Colombian ambassador, his wife,
And their two children—past a carriage driver's
Rusty top hat and brown bearskin rug—
I heard three hundred-thousand-dollar bills
Talking at breakfast. One was male and two were female.
The gray female complained
Of the plantation lent her at St. Vincent
"There at the end of nowhere." The brown stocky male's
Chin beard wagged as he said: "I don't see,
Really, how you can say that of St. Vincent."
"But it is at the end of nowhere!" "St. *Vincent?*"
"Yes, St. Vincent." "Don't you mean St. Martin?"
"Of *course*, St. Martin. That's what I meant to say, St.
    Martin!"
The blond female smiled with the remnants of a child's
Smile and said: "What a pity that it's not St. Kitts!"
The bearded male went for a moment to the lavatory
And his wife said in the same voice to her friend:
"We can't stay anywhere. We haven't stayed a month
In one place for the last three years.
He flirts with the yardboys and we have to leave."
Her friend showed that she was sorry; I was sorry
To see that the face of Woodrow Wilson on the blond
Bill—the suffused face about to cry
Or not to cry—was a face that under different
Circumstances would have been beautiful, a woman's.

HOPE

To prefer the nest in the linden
By Apartment Eleven, the Shoreham
Arms, to Apartment Eleven
Would be childish. But we are children.

If the squirrel's nest has no doorman
To help us out of the taxi, up the tree,
Still, even the Shoreham has no squirrel
To meet us with blazing eyes, the sound of rocks knocked
    together,
At the glass door under the marquee.

At two in the morning
Of Christmas, there is a man at the glass
Door, a man inside the bronze
Elevator. We get off at four,
Walk up the corridor, unlock the door,
And go down stone steps, past a statue,
To the nest where the father squirrel, and the mother
    squirrel, and the baby squirrel
Would live, if the baby squirrel could have his way.

Just now he has his way.
Curled round and round in his sleigh
Bed, the child of the apartment
Sleeps, guarded by a lion six feet long.
And, too,
The parents of the apartment fight like lions.
Between us, we are almost twelve feet long.

Beside the harpsichord a lonely
Fir tree sleeps on a cold
Hill of gifts; it holds out branches
Laden with ice and snow.

Beyond it are paintings by Magnasco,
Ensor, Redon.
These are valued at—some value I forget,
Which I learned from—I cannot remember the source.

Here, from a province of Norway, a grandfather's
Clock with the waist and bust of a small
But unusually well-developed woman
Is as if invented by Chagall.
Floating on the floor,
It ticks, to no one, interminable proposals.

But, married, I turn into my mother
Is the motto of all such sundials.
The sun, shattering on them,
Says, *Clean, clean, clean;* says, *White, white, white.*
The hours of the night
Bend darkly over them; at midnight a maiden
Pops out, says: *Midnight, and all's white.*

The snow-cream my son is dreaming of eating
In the morning, is no whiter than my wife,
And all her lipsticks are like blackberries.
Looking into the cool
Dry oval of her face—snow tracked with eyes,
Lips, nostrils, the gray grained
Shadow of some sorrow, some repugnance
Conquered once, come back in easy conquest—

I read in it my simple story.
Breakfasting among apple blossoms, the first fiery
Rainbow that rings, in spring's and dawn's new dew,
The curly-locked Medusa, I—
                                        I—
To put it in black and white,
We were married.
                        "A wife is a wife,"
Some husband said. If only it were true!
My wife is a girl playing house
With the girl from next door, a girl called the father.
And yet I *am* a father, my wife is a mother,
Oh, every inch a mother; and our son's
Asleep in a squirrel's nest in a tree.

(The mother of one of us
Disappeared while circumnavigating the earth.
The people of a saucer, landing on her liner,
Said: "Take us to your leader."
They were led to the mother.
When she had answered their unasked
Questions, they flew off—and to this day, in another
Star system many, many light-years away,
She governs the happy people of a planet.

My own mother disappeared in the same way.)

That? That is Pennsylvania Dutch, a bear
Used to mark butter. As for this,
It is sheer alchemy:
The only example of an atomic bomb
Earlier than the eleventh century.
It is attributed to the atelier

Of an Albigensian,
Who, fortunately, was unable to explode it.
We use it as a planter.

We feel that it is so American.

Sometimes, watching on television
My favorite serial, *A Sad
Heart at the Supermarket*:
The Story of a Woman Who Had Everything,
I look at my wife—
And see her; and remember, always with the same surprise,
"Why, you are beautiful." And beauty is a good,
It makes us desire it. When, sometimes, I see this desire
In some wife's eyes, some husband's eyes,
I think of the God-Fish in a nightmare
I had once: like giants in brown space-suits
But like fish, also, they went upright through the streets
And were useless to struggle with, but, struggled with,
Showed me a story that, they said, was the story
Of the Sleeping Beauty. It was the old story
But ended differently: when the Prince kissed her on the
    lips
She wiped her lips
And with a little *moue*—in the dream, a little mouse—
Turned over and went back to sleep.
I woke, and went to tell my wife the story;
And had she not resembled
My mother as she slept, I had done it.

She resembled a recurrent
Scene from my childhood,
A scene called Mother Has Fainted.

Mother's body
Was larger, now it no longer moved;
Breathed, somehow, as if it no longer breathed.
Her face no longer smiled at us
Or frowned at us. Did anything to us.
Her face was queerly flushed
Or else queerly pale; I am no longer certain.
That it was queer I am certain.

We did as we were told:
Put a pillow under her head (or else her feet)
To make the blood flood to her head (or else away from it).
Now she was set.

The sound she had made, falling,
The sound of furniture,
Had kept on, in the silence
Of everything except ourselves,
As we tugged her into position.
Now we too were silent.

It was as if God were taking a nap.

We waited for the world to be the world
And looked out, shyly, into the little lanes
That went off from the great dark highway, Mother's
   Highway,
And wondered whether we would ever take them—

And she came back to life, and we never took them.

The night has stopped breathing.
The moonlight streams up through the linden

From the street lamp, and is printed upon heaven.
The floor and the Kirman on the floor
And the gifts on the Kirman
Are dark, but there is a patch of moonlight on the ceiling.

The moonlight comes to the fir
That stands meekly, a child in its nightgown,
In the midst of many shadows.
It has come to its father and mother
To wake them, for it is morning
In the child's dream; and the father wakes
And leads it back to its bed, and it never wakes.

In the morning our father
In his false white, false red,
Took out his teeth and fed them to his reindeer,
False reindeer, and gave us the presents his elves had made
    at the Pole
And gave Mother the money he had made at the Pole—
And explained it all, excused it all
With a cough, the smallest of all small
Coughs; but it was no use, it was unexplainable,
Inexcusable. What is man
That Thou art mindful of him?
A man is a means;
What, amputated, leaves a widow.
He was never able to make the elves real to Mother:
He was a shadow
And one evening went down with the sun.
I have followed in my father's light, faint footsteps
Down to some place under the sun, under the moon,
Lit by the light of the streetlamp far below.

Back far enough, down deep enough, one comes to the
    Mothers.

Just as, within the breast of Everyman,
Something keeps scolding in his mother's voice,
Just so, within each woman, an Old Woman
Rocks, rocks, impatient for her kingdom.

"I have a little shadow that goes in and out with me,
And what can be the use of him I—but that isn't fair,
He is some *use*," a woman in the twilight sings to me.

When the white nun handed to my white
Wife her poor red son—my poor red son—
Stunned, gasping, like the skin inside a blister,
Something shrank outside me;
I saw what I realized I must have seen
When I saw our wedding picture in the paper:
My wife resembled—my wife *was*—my mother.

Still, that is how it's done.
In this house everyone's a mother.
My wife's a mother, the cook's a mother, the maid's a
    mother,
The governess's—
                    why isn't the governess a man?
The things that *I* buy, even,
In a week or two they go over to my wife.
The Kirman, the Ensor, that grandmother's clock
Look by me with their bald,
Obsessional, reproachful eyes, a family
One has married into, a mother-in-law, a—
What is one's wife's mother's mother called?

Do all men's mothers perish through their sons?
As the child starts into life, the woman dies
Into a girl—and, scolding the doll she owns,
The single scholar of her little school,
Her task, her plaything, her possession,
She assumes what is God's alone, responsibility.

When my son reached into the toaster with a fork
This morning, and handed me the slice of toast
So clumsily, dropped it, and looked up at me
So clumsily, I saw that he resembled—
That he *was*—

       I didn't see it.
The next time that they say to me: "He has your eyes,"
I'll tell them the truth: he has his own eyes.
My son's eyes look a little like a squirrel's,
A little like a fir tree's. They don't look like mine,
They don't look like my wife's.
            And after all,
If they don't look like mine, do mine?

You wake up, some fine morning, old.
And old means changed; changed means you wake up new.

In this house, after all, we're not all mothers.
I'm not, my son's not, and the fir tree's not.
And I said the maid was, really I don't know.
The fir tree stands there on its cold
White hill of gifts, white, cold,
And yet really it's green; it's evergreen.

Who knows, who knows?

I'll say to my wife, in the morning:
"You're not like my mother . . . You're no mother!"
And my wife will say to me—
                              she'll say to me—
At first, of course, she may say to me: "You're dreaming."
But later on, who knows?

THE BIRD OF NIGHT

A shadow is floating through the moonlight.
Its wings don't make a sound.
Its claws are long, its beak is bright.
Its eyes try all the corners of the night.

It calls and calls: all the air swells and heaves
And washes up and down like water.
The ear that listens to the owl believes
In death. The bat beneath the eaves,

The mouse beside the stone are still as death.
The owl's air washes them like water.
The owl goes back and forth inside the night,
And the night holds its breath.

BATS

A bat is born
Naked and blind and pale.
His mother makes a pocket of her tail
And catches him. He clings to her long fur
By his thumbs and toes and teeth.
And then the mother dances through the night
Doubling and looping, soaring, somersaulting—
Her baby hangs on underneath.
All night, in happiness, she hunts and flies.
Her high sharp cries
Like shining needlepoints of sound
Go out into the night and, echoing back,
Tell her what they have touched.
She hears how far it is, how big it is,
Which way it's going:
She lives by hearing.
The mother eats the moths and gnats she catches
In full flight; in full flight
The mother drinks the water of the pond
She skims across. Her baby hangs on tight.
Her baby drinks the milk she makes him
In moonlight or starlight, in mid-air.
Their single shadow, printed on the moon
Or fluttering across the stars,
Whirls on all night; at daybreak
The tired mother flaps home to her rafter.
The others all are there.
They hang themselves up by their toes,
They wrap themselves in their brown wings.
Bunched upside-down, they sleep in air.

Their sharp ears, their sharp teeth, their quick sharp faces
Are dull and slow and mild.
All the bright day, as the mother sleeps,
She folds her wings about her sleeping child.

THE ONE WHO WAS DIFFERENT

Twice you have been around the world
And once around your life.
You said to my wife, once:
"Oh no, I've made all my long trips.
Now I'll make my short trips."

Is this a long trip or a short trip
Or no trip?

You were always happy to be different.
You queer thing: you who cooked
Straight through the cookbook; you who looked
As if the children next door dressed you in the attic
And yet came home from Finland fur
From head to foot: today you look regularly erratic
In your great lead-lined cloak
Of ferns and flowers,
Of maidenhair, carnations, white chrysanthemums,
As you lie here about not to leave
On the trip after the last.

Ah, Miss I———,
Hold not thy peace at my tears.

I hear moved—you unmoved, steadfast—
The earnest expectation of the creature
That comes up, and is cut down, like a flower:
"We shall not all sleep, but in a moment,
In the twinkling of an eye,
We shall be changed. When this corruptible

Shall have put on incorruption, and this mortal
Shall have put on immortality,
Then death is swallowed up in victory.
O death, where is thy sting? O grave, where is thy victory?"

The words that they read over you
Are all that I could wish.
If my eyes weren't open,
I'd think that I had dreamed them.
They seem too good for this former woman,
This nice dead thing that used to smile
Like a woodchuck that has learned to smile
When its keeper tells it: "Smile now!"
                                        Where's your smile
Now that the world is disassembling your features?
Is a smile like life,
A way things look for a while,
A temporary arrangement of the matter?

I feel like the first men who read Wordsworth.
    so simple I can't understand it.

You give me the feeling that the universe
Was made by something more than human
For something less than human.

But I identify myself, as always,
With something that there's something wrong with,
With something human.
This is the sort of thing that could happen to anyone
Except—
        except—

Just now, behind the not-yet-drawn
Curtain (the curtain that in a moment will disclose
The immediate family sitting there in chairs)
I made out—off-stage looking on-stage,
Black under a white hat from Best's—
A pair of eyes. Too young to have learned yet
What's seen and what's obscene, they look in eagerly
For this secret that the grown-ups have, the secret
That, shared, makes one a grown-up.
They look without sympathy or empathy,
With interest.

                    Without me.

It is as if in a moment,
In the twinkling of an eye,
I were old enough to have made up my mind
What not to look at, ever . . .

                              If a man made up his mind
About death, he could do without it.
He could shut his eyes
So tight that when they came to wake him,
To shake him and to say: "Wake up! Wake up!
It's time for you to die,"
He wouldn't hear a thing.
                          Oh, Miss I———,
If only I could have made you see it!
If only I could have got you to make up your mind
In time, in time! Instead of someone's standing here
Telling you that you have put on incorruption,
You would have lain here—I can see it—
Encased in crystal, continually mortal,

While the years rolled over you . . .
                                    In my mind's eye
I can hear a teacher saying to a class
About the twenty-first or -second century:
"Children, remember you have seen
The oldest man that ever didn't die!"

Woman, that is.

A HUNT IN THE BLACK FOREST

After the door shuts and the footsteps die,
He calls out: "Mother?"
The wind roars in the leaves: his cold hands, curled
Within his curled, cold body, his blurred head
Are warmed and tremble; and the red leaves flow
Like cells across the spectral, veined,
Whorled darkness of his vision.
                      The red dwarf
Whispers, "The leaves are turning"; and he reads
The dull, whorled notes, that tremble like a wish
Over the branched staves of the wood.

The stag is grazing in the wood.

A horn calls, over and over, its three notes.
The flat, gasped answer sounds and dies—
The geese call from a hidden sky.
The rain's sound grows into the roar
Of the flood below the falls; the rider calls
To the shape within the shades, a dwarf
Runs back into the brush. But smoke
Drifts to the gelding's nostrils, and he neighs.
From the wet starlight of the glade
A hut sends out its chink of fire.

The rider laughs out: in the branches, birds
Are troubled, stir.

He opens the door. A man looks up
And then slowly, with a kind of smile,

Acts out his own astonishment.
He points to his open mouth: the tongue
Is cut out. Bares his shoulder, points
To the crown branded there, and smiles. The hunter frowns.
The pot bubbles from the embers in the laugh
The mute laughs. With harsh habitual
Impatience, the hunter questions him.
The man nods vacantly—
Shaken, he makes his gobbling sound
Over and over. The hunter ladles from the pot
Into a wooden bowl, the shining stew.
He eats silently. The mute
Counts spoonfuls on his fingers. Come to ten,
The last finger, he laughs out in joy
And scuttles like a mouse across the floor
To the door and the door's darkness. The king breathes hard,
Rises—and something catches at his heart,
Some patient senseless thing
Begins to squeeze his heart out in its hands.
His jerking body, bent into a bow,
Falls out of the hands onto the table,
Bends, bends further, till at last it breaks.
But, broken, it still breathes—a few whistling breaths
That slow, are intermittent, cease.

Now only the fire thinks, like a heart
Cut from its breast. Light leaps, the shadows fall
In the old alternation of the world . . .

Two sparks, at the dark horn of the window,
Look, as stars look, into the shadowy hut,
Turn slowly, searching:

Then a bubbled, gobbling sound begins,
The sound of the pot laughing on the fire.
—The pot, overturned among the ashes,
Is cold as death.

Something is scratching, panting. A little voice
Says, "Let *me!* Let *me!*" The mute
Puts his arms around the dwarf and raises him.

The pane is clouded with their soft slow breaths,
The mute's arms tire; but they gaze on and on,
Like children watching something wrong.
Their blurred faces, caught up in one wish,
Are blurred into one face: a child's set face.

THE HOUSE IN THE WOOD

At the back of the houses there is the wood.
While there is a leaf of summer left, the wood

Makes sounds I can put somewhere in my song,
Has paths I can walk, when I wake, to good

Or evil: to the cage, to the oven, to the House
In the Wood. It is a part of life, or of the story

We make of life. But after the last leaf,
The last light—for each year is leafless,

Each day lightless, at the last—the wood begins
Its serious existence: it has no path,

No house, no story; it resists comparison . . .
One clear, repeated, lapping gurgle, like a spoon

Or a glass breathing, is the brook,
The wood's fouled midnight water. If I walk into the wood

As far as I can walk, I come to my own door,
The door of the House in the Wood. It opens silently:

On the bed is something covered, something humped
Asleep there, awake there—but what? I do not know.

I look, I lie there, and yet I do not know.
How far out my great echoing clumsy limbs

Stretch, surrounded only by space! For time has struck,
All the clocks are stuck now, for how many lives,

On the same second. Numbed, wooden, motionless,
We are far under the surface of the night.

Nothing comes down so deep but sound: a car, freight cars,
A high soft droning, drawn out like a wire

Forever and ever—is this the sound that Bunyan heard
So that he thought his bowels would burst within him?—

Drift on, on, into nothing. Then someone screams
A scream like an old knife sharpened into nothing.

It is only a nightmare. No one wakes up, nothing happens,
Except there is gooseflesh over my whole body—

And that too, after a little while, is gone.
I lie here like a cut-off limb, the stump the limb has left . . .

Here at the bottom of the world, what was before the world
And will be after, holds me to its black

Breasts and rocks me: the oven is cold, the cage is empty,
In the House in the Wood, the witch and her child sleep.

WOMAN

"All things become thee, being thine," I think sometimes
As I think of you. I think: "How many faults
In thee have seemed a virtue!" While your taste is on my
    tongue
The years return, blessings innumerable
As the breaths that you have quickened, gild my flesh.
Lie there in majesty!
                        When, like Disraeli, I murmur
That you are more like a mistress than a wife,
More like an angel than a mistress; when, like Satan,
I hiss in your ear some vile suggestion,
Some delectable abomination,
You smile at me indulgently: "Men, men!"

You smile at mankind, recognizing in it
The absurd occasion of your fall.
For men—as your soap operas, as your *Home Journals*,
As your hearts whisper—men are only children.
And you believe them. Truly, you are children.

Should I love you so dearly if you weren't?
If I weren't?
            O morning star,
Each morning my dull heart goes out to you
And rises with the sun, but with the sun
Sets not, but all the long night nests within your eyes.

Men's share of grace, of all that can make bearable,
Lovable almost, the apparition, Man,
Has fallen to you. Erect, extraordinary

As a polar bear on roller skates, he passes
On into the Eternal . . .
                              From your pedestal, you watch
Admiringly, when you remember to.

Let us form, as Freud has said, "a group of two."
You are the best thing that this world can offer—
He said so. Or I remember that he said so;
If I am mistaken it's a Freudian error,
An error nothing but a man would make.
Women can't bear women. Cunningly engraved
On many an old wife's dead heart is "Women,
Beware women!" And yet it was a man
Sick of too much sweetness—of a life
Rich with a mother, wife, three daughters, a wife's sister,
An abyss of analysands—who wrote: "I cannot
Escape the notion (though I hesitate
To give it expression) that for women
The level of what is ethically normal
Is different from what it is in men.
Their superego"—he goes on without hesitation—
"Is never so inexorable, so impersonal,
So independent of its emotional
Origins as we require it in a man."

Did not the angel say to Abraham
That he would spare the cities of the plain
If there were found in them ten unjust women?
—That is to say, merciful; that is to say,
Extravagant; that is to say, unjust as judges
Who look past judgment, always, to the eyes
(Long-lashed, a scapegoat's, yearning sheepishly)

Under the curly-yarned and finger-tickling locks
Of that dear-wooled, inconsequential head.

You save him and knit an afghan from his hair.

And in the cold tomb, save for you, and afghanless,
He leaves you to wage wars, build bridges, visit women
Who like to run their fingers through his hair.
He complains of you to them, describing you
As "the great love of my life." What pains it took
To win you, a mere woman!—"worst of all,"
He ends, "a woman who was not my type."

But then, a woman never is a man's type.
Possessed by that prehistoric unforgettable
Other One, who never again is equaled
By anyone, he searches for his ideal,
The Good Whore who reminds him of his mother.
The realities are too much one or the other,
Too much like Mother or too bad . . . Too bad!
He resigns himself to them—as "they are, after all,
The best things that are offered in that line";
And should he not spare Nineveh, that city
Wherein are more than sixscore thousand women
Who cannot tell their left hand from their right,
But smile up hopefully at the policeman?

Are you as mercenary as the surveys show?
What a way to put it! Let us write instead
That you are realists; or as a realist might say,
Naturalists. It's in man's nature—woman's nature
To want the best, and to be careless how it comes.
And what have we all to sell except ourselves?

Poor medlar, no sooner ripe than rotten!
You must be seized today, or stale tomorrow
Into a wife, a mother, a homemaker,
An Elector of the League of Women Voters.
Simply by your persistence, you betray
Yourselves and all that was yours, you momentary
And starry instances; are falling, falling
Into the sagging prison of your flesh,
Residuary legatees of earth, grandmothers
And legal guardians of the tribes of men.
If all Being showered down on you in gold
Would you not murmur, with averted breasts: "Not now"?

When he looks upon your nakedness he is blinded.
Your breasts and belly are one incandescence
Like the belly of an idol: how can a man go in that fire
And come out living? "The burnt child dreads the fire,"
He says later, warming his hands before the fire.
Last—last of all—he says that there are three things sure:
"That the Dog returns to his Vomit and the Sow returns
    to her Mire,
And the burnt Fool's bandaged finger goes wabbling back
    to the Fire."

Part of himself is shocked at part of himself
As, beside the remnants of a horrible
Steak, a little champagne, he confesses
Candidly to you: "In the beginning
There was a baby boy that loved its mother,
There was a baby girl that loved its mother.
The boy grew up and got to love a woman,
The girl grew up and had to love a man.
Because isn't that what's wrong with women? Men?

Isn't that the reason you're the way you are?
Why *are* you the way you are?"

You say: "Because."

When you float with me through the Tunnel of Love
Or Chamber of Horrors—one of those concessions—
And a great hand, dripping, daggered, reaches out for you
And you scream, and it misses, and another hand,
Soiled, hairy, lustful, reaches out for you
And you faint, and it misses: when you come to,
You say, looking up weakly: "Did you notice?
The second one had on a wedding ring."

May the Devil fly away with the roof of the house
That you and I aren't happy in, you angel!

And yet, how quickly the bride's veils evaporate!
A girl hesitates a moment in mid-air
And settles to the ground a wife, a mother.
Each evening a tired spirit visits
Her full house; wiping his feet upon a mat
Marked *Women and Children First*, the husband looks
At this grown woman. She stands there in slacks
Among the real world's appliances,
Women, and children; kisses him hello
Just as, that morning, she kissed him goodbye,
And he sits down, till dinner, with the paper.
This home of theirs is haunted by a girl's
Ghost. At sunset a woodpecker knocks
At a tree by the window, asking their opinion
Of life. The husband answers, "Life is life,"
And when his wife calls to him from the kitchen
He tells her who it was, and what he wanted.

57

Beating the whites of seven eggs, the beater
Asks her her own opinion; she says, "Life
Is life." "See how it sounds to say it isn't,"
The beater tempts her. "Life is not life,"
She says. It sounds the same. Putting her cake
Into the oven, she is satisfied
Or else dissatisfied: it sounds the same.
With knitted brows, with care's swift furrows nightly
Smoothed out with slow care, and come again with care
Each morning, she lives out her gracious life.

But you should gush out over being like a spring
The drinker sighs to lift his mouth from: a dark source
That brims over, with its shining, every cup
That is brought to it in shadow, filled there, broken there.
You look at us out of sunlight and of shade,
Dappled, inexorable, the last human power.
All earth is the labyrinth along whose ways
You walk mirrored: rosy-fingered, many-breasted
As Diana of the Ephesians, strewing garments
Before the world's eyes narrowed in desire.
Now, naked on my doorstep, in the sun
Gold-armed, white-breasted, pink-cheeked, and black-
    furred,
You call to me, "Come"; and when I come say, "Go,"
Smiling your soft contrary smile . . .
                                        He who has these
Is secure from the other sorrows of the world.
While you are how am I alone? Your voice
Soothes me to sleep, and finds fault with my dreams,
Till I murmur in my sleep: "Man is the animal
That finds fault."
                    And you say: "Who said that?"

But be, as you have been, my happiness;
Let me sleep beside you, each night, like a spoon;
When, starting from my dreams, I groan to you,
May your *I love you* send me back to sleep.
At morning bring me, grayer for its mirroring,
The heavens' sun perfected in your eyes.

WASHING

On days like these
What doesn't blow away will freeze.
The washing flops on the line
In absolute torment—
And when the wind dies for a moment
The washing has the collapsed abject
Look of the sack of skin
Michelangelo made himself in his *Last Judgment*.

Its agonies
Are heartfelt as a sneeze.

When Mama wrung a chicken's
Neck, the body rushed around
And around and around the yard in circles.
The circles weren't its own idea
But it went on with them as if it would never stop.
The expression of its body was intense,
Immense
As this *Help! Help! Help!*
The reeling washing shrieks to someone, Someone.

But as old hens like to say,
The world isn't chickenhearted.
The washing inhabits a universe
Indifferent to the woes of washing,
A world—as the washing puts it—
A world that washing never made.

IN NATURE THERE IS NEITHER
RIGHT NOR LEFT NOR WRONG

Men are what they do, women are what they are.
These erect breasts, like marble coming up for air
Among the cataracts of my breathtaking hair,
Are goods in my bazaar, a door ajar
To the first paradise of whores and mothers.

Men buy their way back into me from the upright
Right-handed puzzle that men fit together
From their deeds, the pieces. Women shoot from
Or dive back into its interstices
As squirrels inhabit a geometry.

We women sell ourselves for sleep, for flesh,
To those wide-awake, successful spirits, men—
Who, lying each midnight with the sinister
Beings, their dark companions, women,
Suck childhood, beasthood, from a mother's breasts.

A fat bald rich man comes home at twilight
And lectures me about my parking tickets; gowned in gold
Lamé, I look at him and think: "You're old,
I'm old." Husband, I sleep with you every night
And like it; but each morning when I wake
I've dreamed of my first love, the subtle serpent.

THE OLD AND THE NEW
MASTERS

About suffering, about adoration, the old masters
Disagree. When someone suffers, no one else eats
Or walks or opens the window—no one breathes
As the sufferers watch the sufferer.
In *St. Sebastian Mourned by St. Irene*
The flame of one torch is the only light.
All the eyes except the maidservant's (she weeps
And covers them with a cloth) are fixed on the shaft
Set in his chest like a column; St. Irene's
Hands are spread in the gesture of the Madonna,
Revealing, accepting, what she does not understand.
Her hands say: "Lo! Behold!"
Beside her a monk's hooded head is bowed, his hands
Are put together in the work of mourning.
It is as if they were still looking at the lance
Piercing the side of Christ, nailed on his cross.
The same nails pierce all their hands and feet, the same
Thin blood, mixed with water, trickles from their sides.
The taste of vinegar is on every tongue
That gasps, "My God, my God, why hast Thou forsaken
    me?"
They watch, they are, the one thing in the world.

So, earlier, everything is pointed
In van der Goes' *Nativity*, toward the naked
Shining baby, like the needle of a compass.
The different orders and sizes of the world:

The angels like Little People, perched in the rafters
Or hovering in mid-air like hummingbirds;
The shepherds, so big and crude, so plainly adoring;
The medium-sized donor, his little family,
And their big patron saints; the Virgin who kneels
Before her child in worship; the Magi out in the hills
With their camels—they ask directions, and have pointed
    out
By a man kneeling, the true way; the ox
And the donkey, two heads in the manger
So much greater than a human head, who also adore;
Even the offerings, a sheaf of wheat,
A jar and a glass of flowers, are absolutely still
In natural concentration, as they take their part
In the salvation of the natural world.
The time of the world concentrates
On this one instant: far off in the rocks
You can see Mary and Joseph and their donkey
Coming to Bethlehem; on the grassy hillside
Where their flocks are grazing, the shepherds gesticulate
In wonder at the star; and so many hundreds
Of years in the future, the donor, his wife,
And their children are kneeling, looking: everything
That was or will be in the world is fixed
On its small, helpless, human center.

After a while the masters show the crucifixion
In one corner of the canvas: the men come to see
What is important, see that it is not important.
The new masters paint a subject as they please,
And Veronese is prosecuted by the Inquisition
For the dogs playing at the feet of Christ,

The earth is a planet among galaxies.
Later Christ disappears, the dogs disappear: in abstract
Understanding, without adoration, the last master puts
Colors on canvas, a picture of the universe
In which a bright spot somewhere in the corner
Is the small radioactive planet men called Earth.

FIELD AND FOREST

When you look down from the airplane you see lines,
Roads, ruts, braided into a net or web—
Where people go, what people do: the ways of life.

Heaven says to the farmer: "What's your field?"
And he answers: "Farming," with a field,
Or: "Dairy-farming," with a herd of cows.
They seem a boy's toy cows, seen from this high.

Seen from this high,
The fields have a terrible monotony.

But between the lighter patches there are dark ones.
A farmer is separated from a farmer
By what farmers have in common: forests,
Those dark things—what the fields were to begin with.
At night a fox comes out of the forest, eats his chickens.
At night the deer come out of the forest, eat his crops.

If he could he'd make farm out of all the forest,
But it isn't worth it: some of it's marsh, some rocks,
There are things there you couldn't get rid of
With a bulldozer, even—not with dynamite.
Besides, he likes it. He had a cave there, as a boy;
He hunts there now. It's a waste of land,
But it would be a waste of time, a waste of money,
To make it into anything but what it is.

At night, from the airplane, all you see is lights,
A few lights, the lights of houses, headlights,

And darkness. Somewhere below, beside a light,
The farmer, naked, takes out his false teeth:
He doesn't eat now. Takes off his spectacles:
He doesn't see now. Shuts his eyes.
If he were able to he'd shut his ears,
And as it is, he doesn't hear with them.
Plainly, he's taken out his tongue: he doesn't talk.
His arms and legs: at least, he doesn't move them.
They are knotted together, curled up, like a child's.
And after he has taken off the thoughts
It has taken him his life to learn,
He takes off, last of all, the world.

When you take off everything what's left? A wish,
A blind wish; and yet the wish isn't blind,
What the wish wants to see, it sees.

There in the middle of the forest is the cave
And there, curled up inside it, is the fox.

He stands looking at it.
Around him the fields are sleeping: the fields dream.
At night there are no more farmers, no more farms.
At night the fields dream, the fields *are* the forest.
The boy stands looking at the fox
As if, if he looked long enough—

                              he looks at it.
Or is it the fox that's looking at the boy?
The trees can't tell the two of them apart.

THINKING OF THE LOST WORLD

This spoonful of chocolate tapioca
Tastes like—like peanut butter, like the vanilla
Extract Mama told me not to drink.
Swallowing the spoonful, I have already traveled
Through time to my childhood. It puzzles me
That age is like it.
                    Come back to that calm country
Through which the stream of my life first meandered,
My wife, our cat, and I sit here and see
Squirrels quarreling in the feeder, a mockingbird
Copying our chipmunk, as our end copies
Its beginning.
                Back in Los Angeles, we missed
Los Angeles. The sunshine of the Land
Of Sunshine is a gray mist now, the atmosphere
Of some factory planet: when you stand and look
You see a block or two, and your eyes water.
The orange groves are all cut down . . . My bow
Is lost, all my arrows are lost or broken,
My knife is sunk in the eucalyptus tree
Too far for even Pop to get it out,
And the tree's sawed down. It and the stair-sticks
And the planks of the tree house are all firewood
Burned long ago; its gray smoke smells of Vicks.

Twenty Years After, thirty-five years after,
Is as good as ever—better than ever,
Now that D'Artagnan is no longer old—
Except that it is unbelievable.

I say to my old self: "I believe. Help thou
Mine unbelief."
                    I believe the dinosaur
Or pterodactyl's married the pink sphinx
And lives with those Indians in the undiscovered
Country between California and Arizona
That the mad girl told me she was princess of—
Looking at me with the eyes of a lion,
Big, golden, without human understanding,
As she threw paper-wads from the back seat
Of the car in which I drove her with her mother
From the jail in Waycross to the hospital
In Daytona. If I took my eyes from the road
And looked back into her eyes, the car would—I'd be—

Or if only I could find a crystal set
Sometimes, surely, I could still hear their chief
Reading to them from Dumas or *Amazing Stories;*
If I could find in some Museum of Cars
Mama's dark blue Buick, Lucky's electric,
Couldn't I be driven there? Hold out to them,
The paraffin half picked out, Tawny's dewclaw—
And have walk to me from among their wigwams
My tall brown aunt, to whisper to me: "Dead?
They told you I was dead?"
                              As if you could die!
If I never saw you, never again
Wrote to you, even, after a few years,
How often you've visited me, having put on,
As a mermaid puts on her sealskin, another face
And voice, that don't fool me for a minute—
That are yours for good . . . All of them are gone
Except for me; and for me nothing is gone—

The chicken's body is still going round
And round in widening circles, a satellite
From which, as the sun sets, the scientist bends
A look of evil on the unsuspecting earth.
Mama and Pop and Dandeen are still there
In the Gay Twenties.
                  The Gay Twenties! You say
The Gay Nineties . . . But it's all right: they *were* gay,
O so gay! A certain number of years after,
Any time is Gay, to the new ones who ask:
"Was that the first World War or the second?"
Moving between the first world and the second,
I hear a boy call, now that my beard's gray:
"Santa Claus! Hi, Santa Claus!" It *is* miraculous
To have the children call you Santa Claus.
I wave back. When my hand drops to the wheel,
It is brown and spotted, and its nails are ridged
Like Mama's. Where's my own hand? My smooth
White bitten-fingernailed one? I seem to see
A shape in tennis shoes and khaki riding-pants
Standing there empty-handed; I reach out to it
Empty-handed, my hand comes back empty,
And yet my emptiness is traded for its emptiness,
I have found that Lost World in the Lost and Found
Columns whose gray illegible advertisements
My soul has memorized world after world:
LOST—NOTHING. STRAYED FROM NOWHERE.
  NO REWARD.
I hold in my own hands, in happiness,
Nothing: the nothing for which there's no reward.

About the Author

The Lost World was Randall Jarrell's seventh and last book of poetry. He wrote four books of criticism: *Poetry and the Age, A Sad Heart at the Supermarket, The Third Book of Criticism* and *Kipling, Auden & Co.;* he also wrote an academic satire, *Pictures From an Institution*, and four books for children: *The Gingerbread Rabbit, The Bat-Poet, The Animal Family* and *Fly by Night*. A lifelong devotion to Chekhov and Goethe led him to translate *The Three Sisters* and *Faust: Part I*. He was a popular and enthusiastic teacher of Literature and Writing at the University of Texas, Sarah Lawrence, Princeton and the University of North Carolina at Greensboro. Jarrell's interests varied from ballet, opera, sportscars, professional football, painting and literature to tournament tennis, bird watching and cats. At different times during his life he was the poetry critic of *The Nation, Partisan Review* and *The Yale Review*. He was Poetry Consultant at the Library of Congress for two years, a Chancellor of the Academy of American Poets, a member of the National Institute of Arts and Letters. His book of poetry, just previous to this one, *The Woman at the Washington Zoo*, won the National Book Award.

In 1965 Jarrell was struck by a car and killed at age fifty-one.

Mary Jarrell has published a number of memoirs about her husband and is the author of *Jerome: The Biography of a Poem, The Knee-Baby* (for children) and has recently edited *Randall Jarrell's Letters*. She lives in Greensboro and shares the home they had with a Morris cat and a miniature dachshund.